Finding Ro-Hun

Ro-Hun Therapy

Awakening Through Spiritual Therapy

Finding Ro-Hun

Cullen McVoy

Pooka Publications
Montclair, N.J.

ISBN No. 0-9640545-0-7

For additional copies of this book
phone (201) 744-5735

To my wife
Elizabeth

Acknowledgments

My heartfelt thanks to Dee Dee Reinleib, the Ro-Hun Therapist in this story, whose contribution can only be appreciated in its reading, to my dear friend Patterson Smith, for his invaluable advice on the design and production of the book, and to my wife Elizabeth, without whom none of this would have happened.

Contents

What Is Ro-Hun?   i

Life Before Ro-Hun   1

First Day   9

Second Day   25

Third Day   34

Life After Ro-Hun   52

What Is Ro-Hun?

Ro-Hun is a new, spiritually grounded therapy for personal transformation. It combines talk therapy, energy work and guided meditation in a unique holistic process. Known as "therapy in fast-forward," Ro-Hun works quickly and the sessions span a short period of time. In Ro-Hun you experience your concerns directly and deal with them immediately. Healing begins on the spot.

An energy-based therapy, Ro-Hun has a solid foundation in modern biophysics. Research shows that the human body is surrounded by a complex system of electromagnetic energy fields. Within these fields human consciousness has a real, physical presence. Human experience is reflected in these energy fields and human behavior is influenced by them. Ro-Hun identifies and works directly with these energy fields to bring about deep and meaningful change.

What Is Ro-Hun?

In Ro-Hun you are introduced to a world of images, sensations and beings that actually live in your energy. These are the creatures of your hidden world within, the things that constantly encourage you, warn you, prod you forward or hold you back. They tell you who you are and what you can and cannot do. You are forever reacting to these energies. You follow them, fear them or fight them, often without even knowing it. In this inner world lie the secrets to your very existence.

In daily life you are scarcely aware of your inner world. At best it is fleeting and illusive. Ro-Hun puts you squarely into this place, with both feet on the ground and eyes wide open (figuratively of course!). There you can look around and clearly see who is there, what they are doing, and how they are affecting you. You can create a new relationship with your inner world. You can nurture the things that help, and make peace with those that hurt.

What Is Ro-Hun?

Once you make contact with your inner sanctum, you can go there any time. It is the source of the answers that have long eluded you. Sometimes referred to as your "higher self," it is the source of your wisdom, creativity and sense of purpose.

Ro-Hun deals with the problematic "selves" that inhabit your energy field. There is your "unworthy self," your "frightened self," your "helpless self," your "judge" and many more. These selves were created in reaction to traumatic events. They are not you, but they are real entities living in your energy. You may see them with arms, legs, eyes and ears, and they may talk to you. Your many selves are not bad entities. They see themselves as the champions of your best interests. But their view of you is flawed or outdated. They guide and protect you with such vigilance that they smother your true desires and purpose.

Your inner selves may appear as characters from a history book. You may see a steel-eyed knight from the Crusades or a potter from ancient Greece.

What Is Ro-Hun?

Whether you believe in "past lives" these characters are in your energy, and are playing a key role in the drama of your life. The knight met a shocking death in battle, so you are still dodging the arrows that menaced his path. Whether they hail from millennia past or your late childhood, they can be discovered and dealt with in Ro-Hun.

Your inner selves carry what we call "faulty thoughts." The unworthy self may say "nobody can love me." The frightened self may say "if I open up I will get hurt." The helpless self may say "I can't do it alone." The judge sits back and criticizes. The judge says "you did that wrong" or tells you you're lazy, stupid or just plain bad. These thoughts may be so deep you don't see them, or so familiar you have forgotten they are there! Once you unveil your many selves and their faulty thoughts, you see how they dominate your daily life. How they crush the budding flower that was meant to be you.

Ro-Hun helps you find your inner selves and their faulty thoughts by bypassing your rational mind. Your rational mind cannot conduct this search because it is using the same faulty thoughts that you are trying to root out. If your logical thoughts are the problem, they can hardly be expected to find the solution.

Ro-Hun bypasses your rational mind by placing you in a deep state of relaxation. You stay fully conscious and cannot be controlled, but you are receptive to your inner voices. You lie face upward on a cushioned table. The therapist talks you through a guided meditation until you become relaxed and calm. Soon you begin to see, hear or feel the inhabitants of your energy field. The therapist helps you describe these energies and how you respond to them. Immersed in the feeling of the energies, you speak from deep within. To your rational mind your words may come as a complete surprise!

It is not enough to know your faulty thoughts, even if you vow to "work on" them. You want to find them, understand their origin, heal them, and release them from your energy. Ro-Hun does this through a systematic process called "thought surgery." You clear your faulty thoughts by healing the problematic selves that carry them. You do this by sending them all your love and compassion. This transforms them, and gives them the strength to leave you willingly. As the problematic selves are cleared, so are the faulty thoughts. The therapist then helps you put positive thoughts and energy in their place.

The therapist also works directly with the energy itself. The therapist's hands touch and manipulate the force fields while you perceive their images. Listen for the crisp sound of flicking fingers. It may be to disperse the energy, gather it together or smooth it out. All to help you explore your energy field and find what you are looking for.

The benefits of Ro-Hun are many and varied. Clients report relief from emotional and physical pain. They see inside themselves in a new way, and find that lost connection with the world around them. But most importantly they find a new capacity for joy and self-love, and a new sense of purpose. Their lives are simply more fun and make more sense.

For example, Julie came to Ro-Hun with two seemingly separate problems; she felt trapped in a bad marriage and was afraid of heights. From the flatlands of the Midwest, Julie had married a successful surgeon, had two children, and moved to a luxury high-rise apartment in New York City. Her husband was both domineering and unfaithful, but she felt she could not leave him. She was also afraid to go out on her own apartment verandah.

When Julie entered her inner world, she found a young girl venturing close to the mouth of a gigantic volcano. Apparently from a past life, the story was that her parents had told her never to go near the volcano. But one day her curiosity prevailed and she disobeyed her parents. She went close to the mouth of the volcano, peered into its deep chasm, and slipped and fell to her death.

What Is Ro-Hun?

Through this story Julie discovered her frightened self, and with it the faulty thought, "if I disobey I will die." From this she understood one reason she had married a domineering man—she needed someone to obey. Obedience to another assuaged her fear of death. And what about her fear of heights? It came from falling into the chasm in the volcano.

With the help of the therapist, Julie sent her love to the frightened self, healed it, and removed it from her energy. Afterwards, Julie reported that within a week she was able to go out on her verandah without fear. Several months later she found the courage to separate from her husband and make a new life for herself. She attributed both events to her Ro-Hun experience.

Sandra, another Ro-Hun client, came with deep feelings of loneliness and isolation. Her relationships with men were few and far between, and although she was an accomplished martial artist and held a good position as a research chemist, her life lacked a sense of purpose and commitment. The first thing she found in her energy was a raging bull. When she examined the bull more closely, it turned into an angry four-year-old girl. The girl was angry because her mother ignored her. Sandra's mother had ignored her ever since the untimely death of her brother. The mother had never recovered from the loss of her son, and had withdrawn from her living daughter for fear of losing her as well. After his death, the mother never spoke her son's name.

From under a cloak of aimlessness and isolation, Sandra had discovered her angry self. The angry self's faulty thought was "my anger will protect me from feeling unloved." This was the key to what was really bothering her; she felt her mother did not love her.

The angry self also had a plan; to curry the mother's favor by taking the brother's place. Engaging in traditionally masculine activities such as the martial arts was one way to step into her brother's shoes. Her femininity took a back seat, and so did romance.

What Is Ro-Hun?

Having unraveled the story of the raging bull, Sandra sent love and forgiveness to her mother and the angry self, healed them both, and removed them from her energy.

After Ro-Hun Sandra began to see her life differently. She found new value in the work she was already doing, and began pursuing interests she would have never tried before. She made a major commitment with the purchase of her own home. A new haircut, jewelry and clothes heralded the arrival of her new found femininity. Also, something interesting happened the day after Sandra's Ro-Hun session. Perhaps it was an extraordinary coincidence, but for the first time in twenty-five years, Sandra's mother spoke her son's name.

Finally, Anton sought out Ro-Hun due to frequent bouts with depression. He found himself in an underground tomb, which turned out to be occupied by his deceased parents. His mother had died in his early childhood, and his father when he was in his teens.

What Is Ro-Hun?

Trapped in this tomb was Anton's dutiful self. The dutiful self had tried to save his parents. Failing this, it vowed to preserve their memory, and with it their pervasive atmosphere of melancholy. The faulty thoughts of the dutiful self included "I must preserve the memory of my parents or I will lose everything." The fear of losing everything was a faulty thought that he had acquired from his father, who was alcoholic.

In healing the dutiful self, Anton released what had become a futile sense of guilt and obligation toward his parents. Instead of pledging his bondage to them, he sent them his love.

After Ro-Hun Anton felt a tremendous sense of freedom and lightness. For the first time he experienced life without a heavy yoke of debt and subjugation. He soon sealed this revelation with a pilgrimage across the continent to the grave of his mother—the first visit since she had passed away.

While Ro-Hun works directly with the body and mind, its greatest healing power comes from the spirit. Ro-Hun taps resources of spiritual

What Is Ro-Hun?

energy, known as universal or unconditional love. This may seem elusive, especially to be harnessed for down-to-earth, life-transforming work. Yet this is the magic ingredient. The Ro-Hun therapist systematically summons this energy and puts it to miraculous use!

Whatever their religious beliefs, Ro-Hun clients often report a profound spiritual awakening. Some hear the "voice of God." Some see beautiful angels or are embraced by them. Others feel deeply cherished by a higher being, or swept up by a powerful force for good. All are overwhelmed by a feeling of love and belonging.

A hug from a high spirit can change your life. Even more if you don't believe in them. One moment you're an isolated body in an inhospitable world. The next you're a magnificent messenger of divine inspiration!

And this is Ro-Hun's message. You are a powerful healer in your own right. The therapist makes Ro-Hun happen, but you are the one who does the healing. The ultimate healer is your own

What Is Ro-Hun?

heart. It is the conduit for universal love. It works its magic wherever your intentions send it. Learn to work with your heart energy, and everything you create has new life and meaning. You are no longer motivated by ambition, duty or fear, but by love. Feel the power of your own healing, and you feel the power of God.

Ro-Hun Therapy was developed by spiritualist Patricia Hayes, founder and director of the Patricia Hayes School of Inner Sense Development, located in McCaysville, Georgia. The basic Ro-Hun procedure is called the "purification." It consists of three, two hour sessions over a period of three consecutive days. There may also be a single follow-up session called a "skim." After that there are advanced procedures for those who wish to go deeper.

Note: The foregoing is from an article by Elizabeth and Cullen McVoy in the *Quality Times,* July/August 1995 Edition, published in New Jersey by Jay Kantor.

Finding Ro-Hun

Life Before Ro-Hun

My life was full. New things I didn't need. A loving marriage, secure job, friends I could count on, two great cats and lots of projects at home. Still, in quiet times I felt like an old pop record, playing over and over.

Don't get me wrong. It was a good tune, maybe even a great one. But what about the tune on other side? I knew there was one, but not sure what it was. I could never just turn it over and play the other side.

With occult things I had an open mind. In fact, you could call me a believer. Now and then I went to psychic readings. I found them helpful and uplifting. "There must be something to it," I

1

thought, as the reader said things about me that could never be learned in the physical world.

Sometimes I had unexplained insights, and would call them a sort of other-worldly event. Some were vague impressions, as behind a thick veil. They were always elusive, just out of reach. Others were like a flying saucer. Came and went without warning—beyond my control. I could never grab hold of them, and make them part of my daily life.

No doubt the other side was there. But it belonged to a chosen few; not me.

My wife Elizabeth was one of them. She always had one foot in another world. I admired her for it and marveled at her insights. But in the household division of labor, I left those matters in her capable charge. That and the book keeping and birthday cards.

Elizabeth first discovered Ro-Hun. In her usual manner she followed her instincts to it. She took a reading from an astrologer named Mary whom she met by chance on the street. At the reading Mary stood up and proclaimed in a loud voice, "Don't you want to get your power back? Get some more joy in your life? You need Ro-Hun!"

"It's like psychotherapy in fast forward," she explained. "The idea is that unhappiness is not just in the mind. It's a real thing that exists as physical blocks in the energy fields of the body. The Ro-Hun practitioner explores the energy fields to find the blocks, and then takes them away. With the blocks gone, so goes the unhappiness. The person comes out with a new sense of lightness and freedom." Mary didn't know any Ro-Hun therapists in the area, but she gave Elizabeth some phone numbers.

Elizabeth picked one of the numbers and called. She got a woman named Dee Dee in Queens. Elizabeth liked the sound of Dee Dee's voice, and asked for details.

Dee Dee said the basic sessions, called the "purification" take about two hours a day for three days in a row. It cost a few hundred dollars, which seemed like a big outlay for something so little known. We thought about it. We could spend that much when the car breaks down, and all we'd get was the same car. At least with Ro-Hun there was a chance of something better, and somehow it seemed worth the risk.

Elizabeth did Ro-Hun in July. She came back happy, and reported fascinating things: images of beautiful angels and guides like ancient Greek Gods. It all seemed lovely, but nothing really unusual for her. That was a wonderful thing about Elizabeth. Visionary creatures were already a part of her daily life.

Then about three weeks after her treatment, Elizabeth had a sudden outburst of uncontrollable rage. I stared at her dumbfounded. It poured out in torrents from the depths of her soul. After that she was a different person. Serene, lighthearted, the weight of the world was lifted from her shoulders. She began to find the answers she needed. She found a new direction in her life's

4

work. It included the study of "Reiki," a Japanese method of giving energy with the hands.

I looked with awe at what Ro-Hun did for Elizabeth. I thought it might help me too, but not nearly as much. After all, she was the psychic one in the family (not me) so she responded more to this type of thing. I expected to go eventually, but not right away. Don't forget the expense and inconvenience. It wasn't easy to schedule a three day trek all the way to Queens.

Then one day—my first sure contact with the other side. In February of the next year, Elizabeth took me to a free Reiki treatment with Roxanne, her Reiki Master. Getting Reiki from across the room, a quivering went through my body and a loud churning in my head. It wasn't a bad feeling, just very strong.

It wasn't a vision or a visitation. Just a feeling. But I could not explain it, and could not deny it happened. No getting around it, I had stuck my little toe into the other side. It was possible for *me*! After that, I would hear a faint, but unmistakable

Finding Ro-Hun

voice in the back of my mind. It told me I was on my way to something new. I could proceed, cautiously of course, to find out what else was there for me.

In March I had a dream. I bought a ticket on April 11, which bore the date April 12. Then I rode in a car across the Whitestone Bridge, and careened off the bridge into the water below. What did it mean? I almost never dream about a calendar date. And a landmark like the Whitestone Bridge? I hardly ever cross it, much less think

6

about it. But the dream was so specific I wrote it all down and marked the dates on the calendar.

Shortly after that I had a severe bout with the flu and an ear infection. "Aren't you a little old to have an ear infection?" said the doctor, prescribing antibiotics and ear drops. The medicine ran its course but the infection went on. The doctor prescribed more rounds of pills of different kinds. "Sometimes it's a hit or miss proposition," he said with rare candor.

Then one night when I emerged from the tub, Elizabeth looked at me with shock and outrage. "You've got spots all over you! Those pills have polluted your body!" She paused a moment, telling herself it was OK to say what she was about to. "Your aura is all messed up with those pills! Don't you think it's time to go see Dee Dee?."

In my weakened and desperate state I called and made an appointment. The three days were Saturday through Monday. Sunday happened to be

Easter. When I hung up the phone I thought of my dream. The first two days of Ro-Hun were April 11 and 12, the two dates in my dream, and to get to Dee Dee I would cross over the Whitestone Bridge!

Then I got a splitting headache. I seldom get headaches and even the flu and ear infections had not given me one. Many times I started to call Dee Dee and cancel the Ro-Hun. Fortunately I held off.

The headache and dream were telling me something. A part of me knew I was going to Ro-Hun, knew it would change my life, and didn't like it! Sure enough, the headache continued until the first day of Ro-Hun, and vanished on my way there.

First Day

The first day of Ro-Hun is here. April 11 is a sunny Saturday. The apple and cherry blossoms are in full bloom on the Van Wyck Expressway in Queens. I exit at Jewel Avenue and pull into a modest, friendly garden apartment complex. More than occasional doubts cross my mind. Can anything deep and spiritual happen in Queens?

Dee Dee opens the door with exuberant greetings. First I see her flashing eyes and big smile. She is small boned and petit, with dark hair and dangling earrings. Her chatty cheerfulness puts me at ease. "How'd you like some tea?"

Finding Ro-Hun

First comes a written questionnaire. Blunt and sweeping questions. Describe your relationships with family in a two inch space (not even a note that you can attach additional sheets if necessary!) But short answers do come to mind, so I put them down and go on. Father: "distant"; mother: "preoccupied." I often felt my parents ignored me in childhood. Older brother: "domineering." He had a critical word for everything I did. Younger brothers and sisters: "no problem." They were much younger; not around during those formative years (when everything that happens hurts a lot and lasts a lifetime). I finish up wondering how three days of Ro-Hun could help with age-old family miseries. Aren't they written in stone by now? Wouldn't it take years of psychotherapy?

Next Dee Dee leads me to a small room. Looks like a typical spare room; on one side a desk with cassette recorder, and on the other a table with a partly assembled model airplane. But most of the floor is taken by a massage table, and an eye-level shelf holds some small crystals and several "thank you" cards. I guess these are from "happy campers" and indeed she points with pride to one from Elizabeth. Still I wonder. Can anything deep and spiritual happen in this little room?

I am told to take off my shoes and lie face up on the massage table. I do, and put my wallet and keys in a shoe. I want to be completely comfortable, and I suppose, free of all worldly responsibility. She puts on a tape of soft, unobtrusive new age music.

Dee Dee begins by telling me to imagine a golden ball of energy at  the bottom of my feet. The energy from the ball flows slowly upwards into my body. As it passes, each part of me relaxes in turn. When the energy reaches the top of my head I feel quite relaxed and serene.

She now asks me to visualize a column of white light. The column goes upwards from my chest, and I rise higher and higher into my inner planes. In a soft, soothing voice she recites grand thoughts of goodness and well-being as I seem to float through the heavens, each time rising to more exuberant heights.

"You are accessing your wisdom, clarity, harmony and capacity for unconditional love. The work we will be doing together is done from your highest, most loving self."

She gives me a wand of light to spread love and joy all around me and throughout my body. As she speaks I sense her moving about the table, first down below my feet, then along my side and finally at the top of my head. I can hear Dee Dee's hands waving briskly above me. At times I feel the wind from their motion. Now I hear a flicking sound from her fingers, as if she's shaking things off.

How long am I suspended in this half-conscious bliss? I don't know, but finally she brings me gently down.

Now things take a different turn. Dee Dee had been running the whole show. She was dishing up generous helpings of wonderment, and I was willingly, but passively partaking. Now it is my turn.

She has a question. "Is there a particular issue you would like to look at at this time?"

For a moment the bliss halts. Who me? I am just here lying on a massage table in a small room in a garden apartment complex in Queens. What could I possibly want to look at now? I draw a blank.

"It doesn't matter," responds Dee Dee in her soothing tone, "Anything that comes to your mind will be fine. Any thought, any sound, anything you see, sense or feel, however fleeting or insignificant."

Trying to oblige, I look hard through my closed eyes. Seeing only murky darkness, I cast about for something to say. "Clouds. Dark clouds."

"Fine," says Dee Dee, without missing a beat. "Now let's shine a bright light on them and tell me what you see."

Doubtfully I pretend to cast some sort of light in their direction. To my surprise, the light catches a quick silhouette of trees. "I see trees with sun shining through them."

Then like magic my view of the trees sharpens. I can make out the outline of palm branches. "Why, they are palm trees!" I'm so relieved to see something clearly.

Dee Dee is right on it. "Let's walk among the trees and see what we find."

Instantly a short, sun drenched palm tree appears before me. It looks so familiar. Of course, it is the tree at the end of our driveway. The one at my childhood home! In Florida we had a small house in the woods next to a swamp full of alligators and mosquitoes. A paradise for a young boy.

Beside me stands myself as a child of six. He is a slight, quiet boy with a distant, questioning gaze. I look at him with detached curiosity.

First Day

"We will all join hands," Dee Dee instructs. "You and I and yourself as a child hold hands and walk up the driveway to your house. We'll see what we find there."

See what we find there? I feel an upsurge from deep inside. I don't know why. Before I can stop I burst into tears. The sunny Florida palm grows dark and the little house appears in the distance. The crying soon becomes a whimper, and the three of us start along the driveway. In the background Dee Dee's waving and flicking continues.

"Now you are standing at the front door," says Dee Dee.

"Not yet, it's a long walk," and I am walking very slowly.

"Some resistance," I hear her say to herself. "Take your time."

We finally arrive at the front door. "Before we go in," Dee Dee directs, "I want you to look into the eyes of this young boy, and send him your love. Tell him that he need not worry, that you have made it, and everything is all right. He can be free to enjoy all the wonder and spontaneity of childhood, knowing that he is going to turn out just fine. I want you to walk over to him, take him in your arms, hold him, and feel the warmth of his love. This warm love lives in you."

I do this, and the tears begin all over again. What a rare opportunity! I can stand in front of this child and show him that he's going to grow up and be alright. His future is protected, so the present belongs to him!

When the sobbing simmers, Dee Dee goes on. "Reach out your hand and open the front door."

I do.

"Are you in the kitchen?" Dee Dee sees the kitchen without my saying.

"Yes. It's the first room on the left as you go in."

"What do you see?"

"It's a small kitchen, barely enough room to turn around. I see cabinets, linoleum on the floor."

"Is anyone in the kitchen?"

"Yes. There is a woman standing by the sink. It's my mother."

First Day

"I want you to walk over to her, and look into her eyes. Tell me what she is feeling."

"Sad. Afraid she is unable to cope. She can't manage her own life, so she doesn't see how she can manage a family."

"Is she nervous?" Dee Dee gets her own sense of it.

"Very."

"Now I want you to hold her in your arms, and let her know you understand her. Let her know you forgive her, and feel her forgiveness for you. Tell her you know of a place where she can learn about happiness and calm, and ask her if she's ready to go there."

Another upsurge of sobbing; then I ask her. "She says yes."

"Walk your mother to the large white column of light." Dee Dee explains, passing her hands above my chest. "See her rising in this column, with many fine threads attached to her and pulling her upwards and out of your emotional body. Faster and faster she rises. Tell me when she disappears into that light."

As she disappears I feel relieved. Somehow I know she will be taken care of. I feel warmly apart from her; not distant or estranged. Perhaps those threads had taken a burden that was once mine.

"She's there now."

"Very good. Now where do you find yourself?" Look around me. "Still in the kitchen."

Dee Dee sounds surprised. "Very well, there must be more for you here. Tell me what you see."

"Same linoleum, cabinets. Oh, now I'm walking to the hallway, standing in front of the heater grid in the floor. The bathroom is straight ahead, the door is open."

"Is your room on the left?" Dee Dee sees it without my telling her.

"Yes. I am going in. It has bluish green stucco-like walls."

"What do you see in your room?"

First Day

Looking around I become alarmed. "Oh no, I see. . . nothing! It's all bare. Not a sneaker, not a shirt. None of my things. Nothing to show I live there!"

"Don't worry. Ask your child self what is bothering him."

"He is raising his arms at his sides with palms facing up. His face is pained. He doesn't know!" My whimpering came back. "He is leading me through the door to the screened porch. That's where my brother and I slept on bunk beds. I was on top. He's telling me he loves this porch; the rain on the tin roof, the frogs in the swamp. It made him happy, but everything else was too difficult, too scary."

"Hold him," Dee Dee jumps in. "Send him your love and waves of golden white light." I can hear her hands moving through the air above my head, and again the familiar flicking sound.

Still sobbing, I hold this little boy in my arms and feel warm energy flow between us. The years seem to fly by, and as they do his body slowly merges into mine. I feel a great sense of calm, knowing that the little boy inside me is happy at last.

Now Dee Dee beckons me to move on. "It is time for you to enter your temple. This is your own personal temple which  houses all that is good about you. Here lies all your powers of love and joy, your spiritual vision and your creative potential. Here resides all of your guides, who are assembled and waiting to be of assistance. Go in and tell me what you find there."

Before me appears a tall, arched entrance with double doors of oak. As the doors swing open, I step into a bright light, like the spotlight in a theater. I am surrounded by a tight circle of identical, Christ-like figures, larger than life. They are motionless, perhaps made of wood, and brightly painted with a high gloss lacquer, mostly the color peach. The figures are dazzling under the bright light. Their eyes are nearly closed, and they hold their hands in front of them in prayer. I look up, and through the circle formed by their gathered faces is a sky of iridescent blue.

"From this day forward, know that your temple is always here for you. Your guides are ready and waiting to assist you. You need only to ask for their help. You will never be alone again. You will forever have access to the highest sources of wisdom and strength."

How wonderful is my temple! Like nowhere else on earth. To think it was there all along and I never went in! Now that I have been there, and caught a glimpse of all it had to offer, I know I will be going back soon.

Dee Dee is speaking. "Now I will leave the room and give you some time to yourself. Just relax and follow anything that comes to mind in this temple."

Finding Ro-Hun

When the door closes, before me stands the image of my father. He speaks to me in a pleading tone. "I may not have told you enough, son. But I love you." I begin to cry again. This time it's a deeper, heavier cry. I gasp for breath and my body begins to twitch and turn. A cathartic sense of release!

Then my mother appears at my father's side, and I put my arms around both of them. We find ourselves back in the little house in Florida. Still in our embrace, we begin to rise into the air. I look down at our property: the house, the palm trees, the driveway and the swamp. It glistens in the sunshine. What a magnificent sight! In all the years at my Florida home I never imagined what it looked like from above.

First Day

We go on rising. Soon I see the woods and pastures around the house, and now the nearby farms. Higher we go, and I see roads, lakes and towns, the whole county. Higher still, and the outline of the Floridian peninsula! We rise swiftly now. The earth becomes a great ball below, and quickly shrinks out of sight. The stars appear all around. In a few short moments, the cramped little house gives way to a feeling of infinite space, unlimited possibilities. What a feeling of release and freedom!

When Dee Dee returns I am in a state of bewildered glee, still sobbing, gasping and twitching on the table. Now we go on with more waving, flicking and wonderful words of well being.

When at last Dee Dee brings me back, all I can say is, "The most powerful experience of my life!" I know I have traveled to another dimension. The things I saw were so real, and so were the feelings! But most undeniable is what I brought back.

When I settle down I feel serene and lighthearted, like the burdens of the centuries have been lifted from my shoulders. In the bathroom I look in the mirror. Is this me? My eyes seem to sparkle. My usually furrowed brow is smooth and still.

What an adventure! And this is only the first of three days. What could possibly happen after this? Little do I know this is just the beginning.

Second Day

The second day of Ro-Hun is Easter Sunday. It is a sunny crisp day, and traffic on the Van Wyck is light. The few people on the road are dressed for church. The air smells of new things to come.

We start with a deep relaxation, and then ascend to the higher levels. Dee Dee asks me to see myself as a ten-year-old child. I do without much problem. There stands a slight young man with a crewcut, arms by his side and legs apart, gazing straight ahead like a cutout paper doll. Then she says to see myself as a five-year-old. I do this too. The paper doll shrinks a few sizes. Then she tells me to see a two-year-old. The paper doll gets smaller still, and chubby. Then a baby. The paper doll becomes a lump with not much shape at all.

25

Finally, she says to see myself as an unborn fetus in my mother's womb.

Wait a minute! Is this possible? I can recall some things as a young child, but before I was born? Wasn't I curled up dumb in a bag of water?

"How does it feel?" she asks, through my unspoken doubts.

Before I can say "nothing" I do feel something. Or is it what I don't feel? I expect to be in darkness, but I'm not. I expect to be warm. I'm not that either. If I can feel anything, I want to feel love. But love is not there.

"Not dark, and I feel no love," I say, surprised that there is an answer at all.

"Look outside. What do you see?"

Outside? First I have to feel something in a bag of water curled up in my mother's womb. Now I have to look through the water, the bag and my mother's womb, not to mention whatever clothes she's wearing, and see what's going on outside? This is nuts. I can't do it!

Second Day

"I see my father." The answer drops out before I know it's there. And there's more. "He's standing there, arms folded in front of him. He's scowling. Not happy."

"Look deeply into his eyes and tell me why he is not happy."

My resistance begins to wane, and I do what I am told. "My birth is limiting him. It's keeping him from some life goal. He's having me because that's what good men do. They have families."

"Now look deeply into your mother's eyes. What is she feeling?"

My mother's face appears close before me and I look deep into her eyes. "She is also unhappy. She's afraid she won't be a good mother."

"Look around you. What do you see?"

I peer to right and left, looking for some object; a house, a crib, anything to show I am being taken care of. "Nothing," I admit. But as soon as I say it, I realize that nothing is something. "Wait, I see wide open spaces, great distances."

Finding Ro-Hun

"This is the space you occupied before coming to earth. You were a light, a consciousness. Now ask, what is your purpose in coming to this life?"

Purpose? My purpose in life? Such a big question! And she asks it like what did I have for breakfast. Like it has a one word answer. "I don't know." Must sound annoyed.

"What's the first word that comes to mind?" Dee Dee keeps at it.

Oh, alright, I'll try. I cast about for a word, any word. "Serenity." That's as good a word as any.

"And how do you expect to accomplish it in this life?"

Now what? She makes me pick a word without thinking about it. Now she says explain the word as if I had thought about it. She knows very well I didn't think about it! I just picked a word because she told me to!

"I don't know."

Dee Dee has no idea how unfair she is. She promptly sets the same trap again. "Just tell me the first thing you see, sense or feel."

28

Second Day

She's wearing me down. I'll try once more, but this is the last time. I press my gaze into the empty space before me.

Then it appears. A sketchy outline, but unmistakable. I see a great bird with wings spread in flight. What's more, this picture of a bird has its own caption. How wonderful! "The bird of freedom! It' me in those wide open spaces, soaring and exploring without restraint. No rules, no bounds, no expectations!"

"Terrific," cries Dee Dee, then she lowers her tone. "Now tell me, what agreement did you make with your parents before you were born?"

What did she say? Unborn child makes deal with Mom and Dad? What is she asking? This is another curve ball of course. But oddly, right now it makes perfect sense.

"Yes, we did agree." I blurt out. Where did this come from? "They would give me lots of room to run free. Let me experience everything, with few demands and few rules. I could choose my own purpose and chart my own course. I didn't want them to smother me with love and attention. That might have controlled me. No blueprints for my future and no smotherly love. I wanted to be left alone!"

"And what would you give them in return?"

This too comes without thinking. "I would be a good boy. Wouldn't take much attention. Let them have their own lives."

Right away I know what went wrong. Tears well up and I gasp for air. The words come down like rolling boulders, laying flat all doubts and confusion in their path. "I really botched up the deal I made. And blamed my parents for it. When they left me alone like they promised they would, I thought they didn't love me!" So simple a child could say it.

In three heart beats I go from horrified, to remorseful, to feeling downright silly. What a shame that I couldn't live with my own deal with my parents. But what a relief that they were just keeping their bargain!

Dee Dee moves on, "Now you have a clearer understanding of your agreement with your parents. So look at them again. How do they feel?"

I look closely into both of their faces. It's like magic. Their whole countenance has changed. "Why, they're smiling. They're happy!"

"Good, now you are going back into that womb, bringing this new understanding. You are ready to be born again." As Dee Dee speaks the flicking goes on in the background. A shiver comes up my spine.

"But this time you will enter the world with only love and joy surrounding you. The world welcomes you as a wonderful new person, as you greet a beautiful new world."

Taken by the intensity of the moment, I prepare myself for this important event. Can this really be happening? Am I going to get another chance? Slowly draw my knees to my chin. Remember this? Of course, the fetal position! Feel the push, push,

push! Moving now. Sliding out smoothly. Resting on the table. Now look around. What a gorgeous world! It's changed; more friendly, more inviting. It seems to want me in it. Here I am, everyone, here I am! I have lots to give now. This time its going to be different!

The end of the session finds me exhausted but happily serene. We talk about what happened, and the agreement that came to light. My mother and father once told me what they wanted for their children. So strictly were my parents raised, they spent their lives breaking the bonds that held them. They would not make the same mistake. They vowed their children would be free to choose their own path. And they did.

Second Day

My heart fills with gratitude for what they gave me. The time has come to accept their gift, with love and without regret.

Third Day

I look forward to my final day of Ro-Hun. Each visit had taken me to places I had never been. The first day left me reeling from a great catharsis; release from the bleakness and desperation of early childhood. The second day took me back before my birth, and what lay at the bottom of my discontent. It captured my thoughts before I was even me!

34

Third Day

On the third day I wonder, where could I possibly go this time? Dee Dee says she doesn't know herself much before the session starts. She finds out by meditating. I guess that means going into a trance and latching onto the first thing that comes to mind. Is that any way to find out anything? Well, it worked for me yesterday when I saw the bird.

First thing when I walk in the door she tells me what's coming. I'm a bit startled. It makes my trip to the womb look like child's play. We will head the same way we did the first two days—back in time. But this time we'll go way, way back. I gulp.

"We will do a past life regression."

Are you sure we can do that? I think but don't say out loud. Do I even have past lives, and if so, could I ever go back and find them? What if I draw a blank? I am afraid, but not of finding something bad. Like the small boy in his room the first day, I am most afraid of finding nothing.

Again we start with the gold ball at my feet. But after that we take a different turn. Instead of rising

35

up into the heavens, she takes me in a downward direction. Down a long escalator, counting backwards from ten to one. Deeper and deeper, down, down, further and further. When we finally reach "one" Dee Dee tells me to step off the escalator.

"You are in a train station. You are standing on the platform, and in front of you is a train waiting to leave. This train will take you back in time, to a life that is important to your life today. Now board the train and take a seat."

I do. It is an old fashioned train with carved oak woodwork and red leather seats.

"Now the train is starting to move. Pulls out of the station, gaining speed. Look out the window as the scenery goes by. Faster and faster the train is going. It's traveling further back in time."

The speed of the train is real to me, but so is a growing sense of dread. What if I draw a bank? What do I do then? I begin to expect the worst. I must have a plan. How do I find something when there is nothing there? I need a clue. Let's see, do I know anything at all about a past life? Ah yes, a psychic once told me I had a life on the sea. It didn't mean much at the time, but it's something. If I draw a blank I'll see water. Maybe Dee Dee will help me from there.

"Now the train is slowing down, slower and slower. It's pulling into a station, coming to a stop. It's time for you to get up out of your seat and walk down the isle to the door." Her voice is so calm, so reassuring. She has no idea the pressure I feel. The moment of truth is here!

"Now step down off the train and onto the platform. Tell me, what do you see?"

As expected, nothing. OK, here goes the plan. "I see wat—. . ." Wait, there is something. Not water at all. "I see sand! Sand all around, and blinding sunshine!" The train did take me somewhere after all! But where? I look out and see something on the horizon. Its stark shape tells me where I am. But I do not believe it, so I hold off saying.

Dee Dee probes for clues. "Look down at your feet. Is there anything on your feet?"

I look down. Sure enough, there is

something on my feet. "Sandals, leather sandals."

"What else are you wearing?"

I look again. The picture is bright and sharp. "Sort of brown burlap, fastened to a leather belt. There are stitches in the leather." Such detail! I can't believe my eyes. I really am in another world!

"Look in front of you. What do you see?"

I can't hold back now. I have to tell her what I saw against the sky. But before I can, Dee Dee asks, "What country are you in? Is it Israel, or perhaps Egypt?"

 She sees it too! "I'm in Egypt," I quickly confess. "I didn't tell you, but when I first got off the train there was a pyramid."

"I see," Dee Dee answers. Her tone says she forgives, but only this once. "What year is it?"

Some numbers flash in front of me. "I see a 13, and some zeros. It's not clear."

"What do you do in this life?"

Third Day

Before me appears a large man. He is dressed in brownish robes with a turban on his head. He looks kindly, and familiar. "I serve this man," I say with conviction.

"What does he do?"

"He herds animals, maybe sheep. He's the head of the herders. He's a man of some wealth, but not social position." To my amazement the information keeps coming. "I serve him."

"Is he your father?"

"No." I still wonder where these answers are coming from. But Dee Dee keeps on asking.

"Do you have parents?"

"No. They died."

"How old were you when they died?"

"Two."

"How old are you now?"

"Thirteen."

"Now I want you to go about your usual day's work, and see what you do."

Finding Ro-Hun

By now I am firmly a part of this young man. I am in his body, and in his world. I do not hesitate to start my day.

"I'm walking down a narrow city street. Buildings on both sides, some large clay pots here and there."

"Is there a market?" asks Dee Dee.

"No." I look around for stands and merchants, but there are none. "The street is not that busy."

"OK, continue to walk," says Dee Dee.

"I'm turning into the entrance of a building. There's a large open room inside. It feels like some kind of church, but I don't see pews, altar or other church-type things. The floor is open, and there are small groups of people around. Maybe they are praying. There is a large stone tablet, twenty feet high, standing in the center of the room. It has writing on it, some kind of hieroglyphics. The figures are a good eight inches high. Some have pictures, and some have bits of color."

Third Day

"Go closer to the figures and tell me what they say."

"The first is a picture. It's the side view of a wagon with large wooden wheels. The spokes are ornately carved. The driver wears a long flowing cape of green and white stripes."

"What more do you see?"

"I see some kind of list. It's rules to follow. Perhaps a code of ethics. There are more pictures." I pause. The first picture embarrasses me. I was going to pass it over, but, what the heck. Who says this regression is rated "PG?"

"It's a man and woman copulating," I say sheepishly, "Maybe this one is about adultery."

Dee Dee chuckles and moves on. "Let's go back to the man you serve. Do you see him?"

He appears again. "Yes."

"Look closely into his eyes, and tell me what he wants you to do."

41

I look, and feel both kindness and great expectations. "He wants me to study the stone tablet, and to spread the word. It's a kind of religion, but more like a set of rules to live by, a moral code."

"What is the message of this code?"

This seems a long question to answer in short, but something does come to mind. "It has to do with kindness, gentleness, forgiveness. These are harsh times. The people are afraid of being conquered by barbarians. They feel they cannot indulge in soft pursuits."

"Do you teach that there is strength in gentleness and kindness?"

"Not exactly. Only that it won't make them weak and more vulnerable to conquest. They live in constant fear."

"Now let's go forward," Dee Dee said, "to a time near the end of this life."

Calm comes over me. "I feel I have lived to a ripe old age."

"Yes." said Dee Dee, "I see a man with long silver hair. How old are you now?"

Third Day

A number comes to me. "I'm ninety-six." Is that possible? That is a ripe old age!

"Look closely into this old man's eyes and tell me what he feels."

I come near to his face and peer directly into his eyes. "Sad." I answer. He did not accomplish what he was supposed to. He has no regrets, but he is sad. He feels his work will not be carried on after his death. He has no family, and no disciples."

"Does he believe in an afterlife?"

"No. When he dies, that's the end of it."

Now I see him on his death bed. The bed is made of small logs lashed together with leather thongs. It is out in the open, nothing around. A large white scarab hangs from a chain around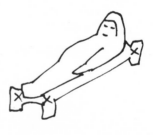

 his neck and rests on his chest. He lies there peacefully looking into a clear sky, waiting to be taken.

Finding Ro-Hun

Dee Dee senses the time has come. "His guides and spirit friends are with him. His work in this life is done. He's made his mark, and others will follow him. He is rising peacefully toward the light." As she speaks I hear her hands moving above my chest, and flicking off to the side.

I begin sobbing again, but with a great sense of peace and contentment. I have returned to my past life and seen my former self. I felt what he felt, and was there for his last moments on earth. A beautiful feeling I will treasure always.

Now to find the train station, and take the long ride back to the present.

But Dee Dee has another idea. "Go back to the church!" she cries. "You must gather the information on the stone tablet and bring it back with you! Continue the work that this man began!"

A chill goes up my spine. I am startled and confused. Is she serious? This whole thing is much like a dream. It's very real to me now; and the feelings of this life are so strong. But like a dream I am sure it will end in a wink, and leave me with nothing

44

but vague impressions and sketchy memories. Is it possible to find real knowledge in this past life? Can I truly bring it back to the present? Will it make any sense at all when this session is over?

No time to dwell on this. There is the stone tablet. It looms above me. I am awestruck. It is bursting with wisdom and truth. Time is short. This is my chance. I may feel silly later. But now I'll take it while I can!

I go up to the stone tablet. How do I do this? Do I just stand here and soak it up through my pores? That couldn't work. Better have a plan. I move to the left side of the tablet. Something makes me look behind it. Oh my, this is not a flat tablet at all. It's a giant cube! And there's writing on the other sides! There must be ten rows of figures from top to bottom.

Really have to get cracking. I go to the lower right hand corner and place my hands on each side of the first figure at the bottom. I press my face close. Once I absorb it I move left to the next figure, staying on the bottom row. It's slow and awkward at first, but the pace improves, as does my confidence. Soon I see the figures speed by before my eyes. When I come to the left corner, I round it and begin the next side, still on the bottom row. Moving more rapidly now.

Around the four sides of the great stone cube I run. The bottom row is done. Now the next row up, and around again. As the frames whiz past I see many things: simple stick figures of men and women, animals, birds, wagons and huts, splashes of greens, pinks, reds and lavenders, intricate symbols of triangles, spirals, circles and grids. They all race by while time stands still. Here is great wisdom and the story of a world long forgotten!

Third Day

Finally I reach the top row, and round the corner into home stretch. I slow down then, and at the last figure come to rest. Catching my breath, I start to tell Dee Dee we can go now.

But something stops me; there is more. I stand up and start across the top of the great stone cube. It is perfectly flat and bare. When I reach the center, I stop and lie down on my back. What am I doing? I can't rest now, and not on this cold, hard stone!

Suddenly I feel a rumbling beneath me. The stone seems to come alive. There are streams of energy rising inside the cube. Starting from around the base, it comes to a point at the center of the  cube's top. The energy rays form a pyramid within the cube. The pyramid's point is right where I am lying. How amazing! The energy comes up through the stone, and straight into the small of my back!

Finding Ro-Hun

Many thin threads in a glow of green light. The rays carry energy thick and potent, like rich topsoil. It enters my back and fills my body. The stream flows on. What a wondrous feeling! This could last me forever! I lie back and revel in its life-giving force.

When all the energy has left the cube, and the last ray disappears into my back, the flow comes to a halt and all is quiet. Now I am truly ready to leave. I tell Dee Dee.

But she still has unfinished business. "You will bring this information back to your present life, and it will be available to you there," she proclaims, as if her words themselves will make it so. "It will be accessible to you through automatic writing."

Now nothing can surprise me or give cause to doubt. My defenses lie in a pile at my feet. Life as I know it has been shaken at the roots. I know nothing of automatic writing, but guess it's done without knowing what will come out. After what has just happened, anything seems possible. I nod with gratitude.

But this is not all. Dee Dee has one final question, and it's a big one, "How are you going to use this information in your present life?"

I could complain about this question. I could say I can't answer without knowing what I am bringing back. After all, I don't know what's in those figures. So how can I possibly know what to use it for?

But I don't say any of that. I hardly even think of it. I just answer the question. "I will use it to help bring male and female energy into harmony."

I have no idea where my answer came from, or what it means. Nor do I know why male and female energy is part of it. But right now it makes perfect sense. It sounds so wonderful, so necessary, so important.

"Good," says Dee Dee, and then announces, "The information is valuable. It will be used for the benefit of all mankind."

She pauses as if to let her words take hold. Then she says in a whisper, "Come, it is time to go back to the train station. Your work in this life is done."

I willingly obey. I have been on a wondrous expedition into another time, and it leaves me exhausted. The train station is a welcome sight.

"The train is pulling up to the platform. It will take you forward in time, returning to your present life. Get on and find a seat. The train is starting to move. Moving forward in time, faster and faster, forward to the present day."

I can feel time speeding by. Decades, and centuries come and go. A homeward race at breakneck speed. Back to the world from whence I came. But which will never be the same.

"Now the train is slowing down," says Dee Dee.

But wait, what's happening? I look up startled. I'm not up to the present. If I stop now I won't be home. I'll be in another time, another past life!

50

Third Day

"Not yet!" I cried, "I need more time to come back all the way!"

"Take all the time you need," says Dee Dee. "All the time you need."

Soon calmed, I let the train move on until the present draws near. "I'm ready now." The train comes to a gentle stop. I sit for a moment on the read leather seat, glad to be back. Then I hop off the train and mount the escalator. Up I go with a count from one to ten. I arrive safely and refreshed at the little room in Queens.

Life After Ro-Hun

　　A different person gives Dee Dee a goodby hug and floats out the door. My steps have more bounce as I go to the car. In the rear view mirror my face is not the same. My eyes, the pupils seem to glow. I'm a new happy man!

I feel quiet inside. Something has left me. My mind is no longer filled with roadblocks—that endless line of roadblocks—obstacles to overcome. Some vanished with a flick of Dee Dee's wrists. Others shriveled away in the light of day. Wherever they went, they're not here now. I have a new way to travel, and the roads are free and clear!

With Dee Dee's skillful and caring guidance, I visited worlds I never knew before. These worlds seem vast, limitless. They go far into the depths of my being; secret thoughts that rule my life without ever seeing the light of day. They reach across continents, and over centuries of time. They harbor the wisdom of the ages and the naked truth about what I live for. These are not hostile worlds to be conquered. They are full of loving helpers, anxious to please and delighted to be noticed. And who would know these worlds are so close by? Don't even have to search for them. I just let them come to me!

Driving back on the Van Wyck, my mind races with anticipation. Can't wait to tell Elizabeth. She never dreamed Ro-Hun would do this for me. She spent years alone in those deepest realms. Now we'll explore the other side together!

And those figures from ancient Egypt; What do they say and what will I do with them? What about automatic writing? Does it really work? Who are my guides? How will they help me?

I lean back in my seat, arms outstretched to the steering wheel. My mind empties and I break into a smile. A little ditty chimes in. I hear it played to a happy tune:

> Life before Ro-Hun is over and done;
> Life after Ro-Hun has just begun.

The Author

Cullen is a New York attorney who for the past twenty-two years has been practicing litigation in the areas of housing, land use and environmental law. He is currently Chief of Litigation for a New York public agency. His experience with Ro-Hun brought about a profound spiritual awakening, and soon after he began trance channeling. Today, in addition to law he practices trance channeling with a spirit named Emmanuel. His wife Elizabeth is now a Master Ro-Hun Therapist, and together they give seminars on Ro-Hun and channeling in the New Jersey area. For more information about Ro-Hun you may call them at (201) 744-5735.